Suzanne Burns

HELL PRESS
UNIVERSITY OF HELL PRESS

Suzanne Burns

HƎLL PꓤƎSS
UNIVERSITY OF HELL PRESS

This book is published by University of Hell Press
www.universityofhellpress.com

Cover and Interior Design by Olivia Croom
http://bit.ly/oliviacroom

Published in the United States of America
ISBN 978-1-938753-25-1

Girls,
I know you will understand this
and feel the intrinsic, incredible emotion.
You have just pulled over your head the worn,
warm sweater belonging to a boy...

—Cadell Meryn, *The Sweater*

This book is dedicated to my two favorite Es:

Eve Connell, the best editor a girl who writes poems about boys could ask for,

and in loving memory of Edie Zukauskas; wherever she is, she knows why.

CONTENTS

PART ONE

The Best Things in Life
Make You Sweaty

FIRST BLOOD

On the back porch
our black clothes
leaned into each other in a way
that almost meant something,

too young to know much
about werewolves,
too young for R movies,
too young to watch
Griffin Dunne far from London
forgetting to stick to the road

as you pretended to pin me in the dark,
the smell of you so different
from the smell of girls
You reeked of anticipation,
danger and Doritos
as you growled in my left ear
before asking me
to bite you like a vampire.

In those days vampires and werewolves
never hung together,
never shared the same movie stage,
fur and fangs so disparate
in our teen games of sneaking
Anne Rice under the covers,

but I already knew we were spending
our last full moon together,
pretending Friday night
would stretch on,
the eternal wish at sixteen
for nothing but more time

because we grew up fast,
our words and our cars
and our boys moving so fast
I pushed my teeth into your neck
to stop what felt like a toy
spinning just out of reach,

my baby teeth only a few years lost,
quarters from the Tooth Fairy spent
on gum I chewed into the shape
of each new dagger to shore up
the tight blood hole that hurt to tongue.

LOVE IN REVERSE SKATE

My round body somehow knew
how to skate better than the skinny girls
who clung to the roller rink wall
in a tight-jeaned, barrette-wearing pack
waiting for you to play Joan Jett.

How I worshipped the freckles
burned along your arms
as the disco ball dropped
from the ceiling during
couples skate, even better
than Donny Osmond's burnished skin
on the cover of the album where he sings
about lollipops, lace, and lipstick.

How I skated by you,
transfixed that you knew
all the words to *Pass the Dutchie*
and could lip sync while
rolling backwards,
and how you almost asked me,
one time after my loyal years
following you around the rink
each Saturday,
to skate a slow song with you
until a little girl tripped
and you had to administer
first aid and free balloons

so I skated with another boy
who didn't want to hold my hand
during *The Piña Colada Song*
and I wondered how many other boys
I had to get past to get back to you,
and if love meant floating around
in circles until the right boy caught up.

How I loved the way you ate
a strawberry Charleston Chew
on your break, biting off the edge
of the wrapper with your buck teeth,
spitting the red paper on the floor,
that tiny torn heart the other girls
skated over while I ached
to pick up any part of you
to carry around in my back pocket,

something you had touched,
the psychometry of my left butt cheek
divining how much you longed
for me in private, under the covers
upstairs where you lived,
and how someday you'd ask me
to stay after the last couples' skate,
the skinny girls paired off
with the skinny boys waltzing
their clumsy, heavy wheels
around and around to Air Supply
or Foreigner or Van Halen
after David Lee Roth removed

his back from the record machine
and someone else took his place.

SERENADE

Sophomore year I carried around
a lunchbox I spray painted black
one summer break
and the yearning to be Juliet,
the poison, the dagger,
the girl with the boy outside
her bedroom window
calling her the sun until
the night I heard rocks
tapping my glass.

A sound like hard rain
awakening the storm
that rested between my ribs,
lightning ready to flash
a Morse Code of longing
to be a girl who knew
a boy ardent enough to gather
pebbles in his swift hand,
a call of action from you to me
to rise up, to be ready

as you sought out my window
glowing in pink teen light
where I tossed myself to sleep
with the knowledge
of all heartbreak to come
under a fluffed canopy

of flowered sheets
and the matted fur
of a favorite stuffed animal
with so many secrets to keep.

BIG NOSE

Part 1:
Our mothers warned us
about California boys
the year we tilted our noses
away from the magazine smell
of Corey Haim in *Tiger Beat*
to the Technicolor glow,
such yellows and golds,
of real-life SunIn.
All those peroxide bangs we
longed to tangle our mall bangs in.

California boys
could tune in the one station
that played *Shake the Disease*
on Friday night repeat
while we waited
for our Top 40 call sign
to lose its static,

while I waited for you
to look up from your guitar
long enough to notice
I could be more
than your girlfriend's best friend.

She with hair from *Seventeen*
who went through life

sucking down free milkshakes,
her button nose sewn
to the exact middle of her face
while my Roman profile
bullied its way into every room.

A nose like the nose of a man
on the cover of *Time*
during the Gulf War,
and didn't you laugh
as you show-and-told your way
through the day comparing
my photo to his,

Central Oregon's only sand nigger,
you said,

and didn't she laugh, too,
knowing, in 1991,
I was cast in our play
as the ugly one.

In the bathroom after last period
I let my tears propel me.

Finally, something to cry over,
a small town, small school,
small-halled injustice
while your band practiced
Smiths' songs in the music room,

while a friend of a friend
passed me a note
to ride the afternoon bus
one stop past my house to you,

with your mom who worked downtown,
with your father who for Christmas
brought guns and CDs from L.A.
Black and white checkered Vans.
Laser discs big as dinner plates.

I ignored your request
and sewed black ribbon roses
on Goodwill sweaters, inhaling the air
of late spring, when it almost didn't matter
that I was the before picture
for rhinoplasty.

Part 2:
The Friday before Prom I came over.
At your house, my best friend
asked for advice on dresses
as we waited in your room,
on boutonnières,
on how many muscle relaxants
would pour her body
out of the dance and into your arms.

She offered to go for pizza if I paid,
girls with big noses

trained to always carry cash,
so I waited for you as her blondeness
impressed itself down your driveway
and you returned from wherever
handsome boys spent their afternoons.

In your room I arranged my hair
on your pillow in a fairytale braid
almost strong enough to climb
and counted your Swatch watches
in the twilight heat,

pretending to sleep
as the song you hummed entered
my daydreams while you, in real life,
band practice over a few minutes early,

strummed your guitar
at the edge of your bed,
the taut-stringed tendons of your arms,
your legs folded under
when I let one eye peek.
Like a painting called
The American Dream
you sang a Southern radio song
all the college stations played.

Your voice the deep register
singing about losing your religion
to a face lost in its own asymmetry

until you leaned in to kiss
the tip of my nose,
your eyes closed,
then danced your fingers
across my forehead
as if checking for a fever
just ready to break.

LUNCH DATE

Maybe because you
never brought a lunch
and maybe because
you sat in the cafeteria
watching all the boys
shove past you
for burgers and fries

while the girls who never
seemed to do their homework
but moved to the front
of every line
crowded around the salad bar,

our school the only one in the district
daring to experiment
with cherry tomatoes and baby corn,

with the option of chocolate milk
for two quarters,
with the option of boys
who never brought their lunches
sitting at a table, hungry,

I packed an extra sandwich
just for you.
My daily offering placed
by your side as you perched
close to me, no questions asked,

your leather jacket
whitened at every crease,
always smelling warm,
an animal heat,
something nearly inviting,

your cousin at the next table
who always tried to sneak
his pet lizard, snake, spider
into science class,
me trying to understand
why you never wore boots
when it snowed and why
you never carried any books

but passed me notes in the hall
with Cure lyrics scribbled inside,
Fire in Cairo a favorite
with its rhythmic chorus
almost like a cheerleader chant

sung by a tenor in another country
whose tessitura always leaned
towards benevolent Goth,

who understood the circles
under your eyes as you reached
for the peanut butter and jelly
while I stared at the worn collar
on your flannel shirt,
your faded cuffs,
your missing button.

POET

After you moved to Florida
you wrote each of us love letters,
three friends you sent
long white envelopes filled
with Southern news that read
so special in your sloppy hand
compared with our Western news
of the one record store in town
deciding to carry the new Cure CD
and even a 12" to follow.

We wrote you about rushing home
to turn on our stereos, a mad dash
to be the first in our mope rock world
to pretend Robert Smith was singing to us.

You're missing all the good stuff,
I wrote you, *all the best rituals,*
and you sent back poems.

Short poems about love and longing
close to the ones you sent my friends,
us comparing you with delight
as we huddled in a velvet mass
the next day at school.
Earnest poems with misspelled words
my sister pointed out with no appreciation
for me knowing a boy who sent love poems

the same way one of my boyfriends
pointed out a misspelled word
in a poem I wrote for him.
Characoal, he said, *has an extra "a,"*
his thin finger smearing the word
on the notebook paper I'd folded
in fourths and sneaked him
in our first period writing class.

Charcoal, I repeated the rest of the day,
charcoal, charcoal, charcoal
until all I could see
as I listened to my Walkman
under the covers before bed,
that one sad song from Xanadu
no one knew I had memorized
night after lonely night,
were streaks of charcoal
behind my closed eyes.

I regret that I never sent you
back an attempt at a love poem,
something about a lonely breeze
surprising me on a warm night,
something about your mouth,
something about life, me too shy
to ask if you remembered
the afternoon you danced for me
in the living room as we waited
for the Jell-O chocolate pudding
to set in the fluted glasses,

four servings though you knew
I'd give you two
when no one was looking,

and boy how you danced to INXS,
an old record we bought
for a quarter downtown,

your long brown hair the sort of hair
too dangerous to touch,
bobbing to the melody in a way
where we never could imagine
you'd move away and leave any of us.

PEN PALS

You never noticed me until
your childhood friend
from Washington wrote a letter
to you after Christmas break

and a few letters to me.

At sixteen I understood stationery,
my signature color, red.
Red paper, red envelopes
in a neat pile on my desk
with my Poison perfume
never too far away
for a tasteful purple spritz.
Stamps I picked out
from the black binder
at the post office downtown

when girls wrote letters to boys

after Christmas vacation
until at least spring break,
our bubbled handwriting
crossing paths with their small,
leaning in on itself boy cursive
we stalked our mailboxes to find
waiting behind the metal doors,

ugly little letters
on boyish yellow paper,
over-folded, fingerprinted,
stuffed in small white envelopes,
nothing fancy or thick,
few words, never about us
or the weather or the times we had

but letters about them,
our pen pals from lands
as far away as Idaho,
the friend of a friend boys
who came to town to ski
or eat turkey with their moms
and stepdads before waiting
for that glorious call
to escape in the nearest car
with Dead Kennedys on the stereo,
Give Me Convenience
or Give Me Death
as you and your friend
drove the two-street downtown
in search of something past
the flurries of snow,
the last-minute Christmas gifts,

only to see me in a café
sipping hot chocolate with a girl
too in love with Jesus for her own good,
a girl I passed the time with the way
I've always passed time with girls—

until the next boy shows up.

Your friend needed to know
what kind of girl drove to town
just to drink hot chocolate
in a tall, handled, glass mug,
tanned with too much steamed milk
when the only café in town
put steamed milk in everything

and I waited for the two of you
to notice how I was different than the girls

who drank coffee at Denny's
and sat too close to boys in that way,
needy and obvious,
swearing when they swore,
mixing too much pepper
with ranch dressing
to eat fries the way boys
ate fries instead of the way

the girl in love with Jesus
and I ate fries,
though we never wanted
to smear our lipstick so
never really ate anything at all.

I waited and your friend noticed,
asked me to a movie,
sat close to me and laughed

whenever I laughed
and almost held my hand,
his hand so large,
while you tried to see
what he found so sexy in the way
I knew you sat behind me
but never looked back.

I refused to look back
though I felt your eyes
burning on my neck,
unable to predict the mess
we'd get in down the line,

the blood you left
on my front porch after
that one bad night.

The ambulance. The move.

The shared eyeliner.

The letters he wrote me
that I showed you when
we still spoke.

The letters from Washington
long after Santa
left his cookie crumbs behind
and I lingered for the mail
as if each day was Christmas

and you sat in your room
down the street waiting
for someone to write you back.

DAN FROM CALIFORNIA

We all wanted to be your girlfriend,
Goth boys from Southern California
hot properties in Central Oregon
with their structural hair
and their trench coats
and the way they knew all the words
to every song by every band
on the college radio stations except R.E.M.,
because who cared about a band
everyone else liked, too.

You knew Depeche Mode
like the back of your light brown hand,
your Mexican skin so exotic
against our solid white foundation
as we imagined your hand touching
our porcelain doll hands,
your culture as foreign as the way
you stood from our couches
when one of our mothers entered the room.

Your mother lived under the railroad tracks
near the Army surplus store alone, the one
who assembled earrings for money,
the one who invited me over
one Saturday to help decorate your room
then paid me in earrings that didn't match,
the glass beads arranged in patterns

that changed colors as I held
each bangle up to the light.

You dated one of us
when you showed up our senior year
and me before you moved away,
with a few more in between
Homecoming and Prom.

Each one you kissed and touched
in ways no boy in Central Oregon knew how,
you with an ex-girlfriend
who wore a spider web tattoo
on her left breast
and *USDA Choice* branded on her ass
and I wondered
how many asses you had seen,
how many breasts
in your short Venice Beach life

where you posed
in a striped, long-sleeved shirt
like Corey Feldman's lost brother
waiting to get the Frog brothers
back together.

Each one of them you kissed,
and touched, but not me.
There was something about me
beyond kissing and touching, you said.
Like I was someone you wanted

to know, to eat dinner with,
to watch your mom teach
how to string beads.

You wrote me letters
when you lived in town
and even one or two
when you moved back to L.A.,
letters that never revealed much.
Letters I read two hundred times each,
the hunt for secret meanings
behind every word.

Because you had no money
to buy magazines,
and I told you how much
I loved magazines,
you decorated the envelopes
with your beloved cassette covers,
miniature square posters you cut out
and taped under my name,
more sacred than if you'd sent
me a diamond in each one,
and I wondered for years
if you thought of me
as you thumbed through
your music collection
trying to figure out
which empty case to choose.

PART TWO
The Old (Community) College Try

MY FIRST PROFESSOR

College girl bored with college boys
who pretended to understand
how to move that piece
that looks like a horse in chess,
I climbed fast past all the other girls
with my lipstick and my poems
and my need to believe in you
because you believed in Sylvia Plath.

On breaks from my part-time job
I practiced licking ice cream cones
down to their cold center roots
as I imagined each freezing knob
to be a sweet tooth
you bragged about during finals.

You who came to class dressed
like a man, with a brown belt
and shoes that matched.
You dressed like my dad
and every other dad,
but drove a little red car,
Nine Inch Nails sticker on the back.

You were only twenty-nine.

You kept me once after school,
not to touch my lips

or unbutton my dress
but to sneak me a chocolate bar,
the ordinary brown wrapper
with the stunning silver underslip
I folded and kept in my copy of *Ariel*,

or maybe you kept me after class
to critique my poems and I clung
to the good words and the bad
and I sat close enough to see
the variegations of light
in your long, dark hair
and that one tag ball
on your sweater vest.

I loved you the way a schoolgirl
loves her first English professor,
pornographic, inappropriate love
mixed with wanting to hold your hand
all the way through a movie
J.D. Salinger love mixed
with hoping nobody caught me,
and everybody caught me

in your office, all the pretty girls
you didn't seem to notice,
the ones who understood
the beauty tips in magazines,
the other ones who wore no makeup
but read all the right books,
all the students who wanted

a piece of you as we broke off
piece by piece of that candy bar
and passed the fleeting sweetness
back and forth until your next class.

BEACH DATE

Our first time at the ocean,
old enough to afford a view
but young enough to order
baked potatoes from Wendy's
and eat dinner on the hotel bed,
intoxicating mess
of cheese and sour cream,
green onions dropping
like stinky jewels between the sheets,

Pedro on *The Real World* dying of AIDS,
us glued to the screen before
our small town realized
how much it wanted its MTV,

before we realized how two people
need to want to stay together
to stay together,
our talk of marriage nothing more
than occasional static between
commercials for flavored lip gloss.

When you fell asleep,
always before me,
your head seeking the pillow
I wanted to fight you with,

to throw at you,

to see if a cloud of feathers
really waited beneath the stiff slip
like in horror movies
when girls wallop each other
with pillows while they wait
to become victims,
the atmosphere, the scene
overtaken with those slow-motion
feather bombs,

because I wanted to be your victim
because I wanted to be something
to somebody but kept picking boys
who fell asleep too early,
even years after the baked potatoes,
even years after Puck stuck his fingers
in Pedro's peanut butter,

years before everyone
lived their lives on screens
so we have no pictures
of our potatoes or our pillows,
of you finding your way into dreams

as I tucked my legs under my body,
perched on a hotel chair beside you,
and searched for something in the air
close enough to reach.

THE PROPOSAL

Part 1:
I'll never know if adventure
pulled you from me, or the promise
of better drugs in bigger places,
but you arranged your final afternoon
to charm my suitcase out of the closet

in hopes you could coax away
my dark ruffles, my Mary Janes,
tread worn from circling
the two-block downtown radius
always in search of something.
Anything.

And didn't we transform those blocks?

Didn't we infuse them with as much magic
as we knew how, while everyone else
stood in line to hear Michael Damian
sing *Rock On* at the mall food court
or buy tickets at the fairgrounds
for donkey basketball?

We smoked a clove against a bike rack
the Friday night before you moved away,
our teen leanness curving
into a definition of irony

we never understood
under that one streetlight,

the exotic rush of mid-summer moths,
a bottle of Heineken someone stole,
the payphones we dug our painted nails in,
a quarter for the night a worthy,
shared achievement

before we forgot the prize
in another black pocket
and you kissed me so hard
something about your lips
scared me away from you
before I knew how much
I love to be scared.

The Friday night
before you moved away
we took turns reciting *Kubla Khan*
in each other's ears,

the measureless caverns,
the sunless sea,

the same way you translated
foreign movies, your soft words
getting lost in the thicket of my hair
because I refused to wear my glasses,

(Remember the Japanese one
about noodles?
The French one about the husband
whose wife is too beautiful?)

and you thought your translations,

this poem,

meant I would follow you anywhere,
and how my large eyes let you believe
anywhere would be good enough.

Part 2:
The day you left you knocked
on my back door with a gift,
a record wrapped in blue paper,
music the secret language between us,
a lily tucked between the folds.

You never gave me flowers
because of the stories
of boys who came before you.

Boys with red roses
and chocolate-covered potato chips
in small white boxes
from the candy store downtown.

Boys with black roses dipped in ink
stolen from the art teacher.

Boys with daisy bouquets
that smelled like the apologies
on my front porch the morning
after each new teen tragedy.

Your lily curved
like the inside of your white ear,
your ears so clean,
always tasting of Aquanet,
the big blue can
that turned your hair into architecture
before the sky rejected your aerosol,
before I rejected your proposal
as you handed me the white flower,
our white flower,

calla,

its thin, gold tip curved into a question.

Lily, because I was born
in the month of the lily
and my name means lily
and you are the only one,
even now,
with all the poets I have known,
to figure out this basic equation.

And isn't it strange how
when you put on the record,
its blue paper crumpling

beneath our boots
the way your sheets
once crumpled beneath me

the winter all we did was listen
to Lou Reed and your radiator
speaking to each other
in that register we told ourselves
could only be understood
in New York,
our big plans to buy our fathers
fake Rolexes,
share a hot dog at Coney Island,

you gripping my waist
in an improvised waltz,
your velvet shirt
stuck to my velvet shirt,
your talk of marriage
as we tried to keep time
to a slow cello,
to one piano,

I thought that one lily,
my lily,
would be the beginning
of so many other lilies.

So many I might
press them in books
or dry them upside down,

a row of pale, fragrant bats,
or give them away to nursing homes,

lilies marking my life
like punctuation
at the end of every sentence.

So many lilies
I wouldn't have time for you,
alive in my white petals,
the yellow middles
arced like statuary,
so I asked you to leave,
to take the memory
of your cigarettes and your hairspray
and your proposal,

all those nights we tried
to turn our small world
into something bigger,
something you set out to find,

alone,

something you promised to write home about.

ARMY BOY

You asked me to go dancing
the night I wore low-rise jeans
to your poetry reading
with a black thong
that only showed on my right hip
and only when I moved a certain way.

You read something about wearing
a towel as a Superman cape
when you were a boy.

You were from Yuma, Arizona
so you called yourself *Yuma, Arizona*

and didn't know we lived in a town
where no one goes dancing.

Out of the Army before Iraq,
still an Army Man
like my Navy father warned me about,
we shared pizza on the floor
of my living room, missing
its couch between boyfriends,

Warren Zevon dying on Letterman,
Roland the Headless Gunner on a TV
missing its stand, everything that night
trying to create a new word for *temporary*.

When you told me you saved
your Army checks in Italy
to buy a tiara for the first girl
who resembled Audrey Hepburn

I wondered what you were doing,
sitting next to me and my thick thighs
and my ambition to be more
than a girl waiting for a boy
to buy her diamonds.

We talked about books over coffee,
another poet with a dimpled chin
and dreams of hitching your lonely,
wandering the countryside
in search of the perfect slice of pie
and the perfect farmer's daughter
poems to mine,

all out of pies and daughters
as you gave me a picture
of yourself posed in a field,

almost like James Dean,

but not enough to make me
get up off the floor in search
of tacks or tape,
in search of a way to hang up
your photograph in a room
missing all its other photographs,
missing all its other boys.

LONG TERM

You left me in the car
for two hours while
you visited an ex-girlfriend
who lived in an apartment
somewhere in Tigard.

Sheena of the fabled leopard bikini
who hot tubbed with you
in eighth grade,
who broke up with you soon after.

Who changed your personality.

Who made you see a psychiatrist
who recommended you try Prozac
so instead you sought out girls
dumb enough to wait for you
in a car on a rainy afternoon

six years after your breakup
while you tried to figure out
if you wanted to stay with me
or go back to her.

She of the catastrophic leopard bikini
who didn't want you anymore

and I never even honked the horn
or turned off the windshield wipers
that caught, and then moved
into the rhythm of my tears

because waiting for a boy like you
was supposed to mean something
more than waiting

so we moved in together
and tried to combine ourselves
and you let me sit on your lap
when the cat died
and I changed your bandage
when your arm fell
into the deep fryer at work.
I helped you sharpen your knives
and we listened to your records
and we talked at night,
in the dark,
about your crazy aunt
sometimes

but these little details
failed to create a life
whether or not we took
ironic photos at Sears
dressed in red flannel for Christmas
and signed both of our names
on every card

and waited for cards to come
back, to tape to the wall
in the shape of a star,

a shape that even shined
when we turned off all the lights.

PART THREE

Two Poems That Are Sort of
about Cheerleaders
But Are Really Still about Boys

BREAKUP IN SHARI'S
PARKING LOT

In high school you were on
the five-year plan so everyone
warned me to stay away
from your big black boots
and your hair dyed Bauhaus black,
Rose Garden Funeral of Sores
a familiar dirge on your tape deck
as we passed afternoons hunting
for thrift store treasures
long before DIY crafts became the thing.

Sometimes we shared lunch downtown
while the student body president,
another profile somebody,
ate at a distant table cloistered
with the student council
as if we were the small dark mass
they planned to annihilate
at the next pep rally.

This made us feel tight,
this you and me against the school assembly
where everyone seemed to know
what they cheered for, such fervor
of support for the home team,

Go, Fight, Win!

the cheerleaders and Germaine Greer
on opposite sides of the cosmos
with their panties showing
as they did splits, with their tight
yellow and blue sweaters,
with their skirts whose length
was never to be blamed for date rape,

but didn't help,

the one who slept with the quarterback
and got a Coke bottle stuck up inside her,
the one who flirted with the Goth boys,
the one who swore Karen Carpenter
was her godmother as she stuck
her finger down her throat before each game
while after school you and I made
macaroni and cheese together out of the box
and didn't even add our own touch

because we already were our own touch
that nobody else could get close enough
to break up until the night
someone saw you getting into that car
in the Shari's parking lot

so my friend drove me
to the Shari's parking lot
and she and I watched you sitting

in the front seat of another girl's car.

Wendy with the ordinary name
and the yellow hair
and the mall clothes.

Wendy who you felt sorry for
because cream in her coffee
made her remember being molested,

that thick, white omen
swirling on top,

her tears you always seemed to be
in the right place to wipe away
though she didn't see you *that way*,
and she *was old news from before.*

Wendy who you felt sorry for
because you couldn't feel sorry for me.

I smiled too often.
I wore new shoes.
My mom signed every field trip slip on time.

And as my friend and I sat
in the incensed warmth of her car
we watched you, my boyfriend,
kiss Wendy in the front seat,

your pale, insistent hand

on her normal chin, our Sylvan town
fire-lit from your eyes on hers,

Go, Fight, Win!

that kiss meaning I had no one
to hate the cheerleaders with,
no one to mix tapes for,
no one's dark cloud
to add to my dark cloud
until, cloud to cloud,
we felt a storm brewing on the horizon

that you had promised me
with your Misfits tee,
a black and white skulled invocation

no ordinary girl could ever clear.

SECRETS

I was the one she liked,
the red-haired cheerleader who,
after high school, ditched
her pom-poms for velvet leggings
and that green velvet shirt,
walking autumn as she went
from college class to class
and your black turtleneck followed,

my boyfriend with the wandering eye
able to assess each girl in your path,
the ones from farm towns
with symmetrical faces
who practiced wearing
red lipstick for the first time.
The ones from Portland who
had already seen all the good movies.
The one in drama class who ran lines
from *Uncle Vanya* in the commons at lunch

while the former member of the Varsity squad
licked tzatziki off her fingertips
as we ate peanut butter sandwiches
and still drank milk.

Me with the unusual face and the nose
big enough to cut off and spite myself,
and the priest's underclothes

I bought for two dollars
at the Catholic thrift shop, creamy,
scalloped lace embroidered in crosses
I wore peeking beneath a black smock
that seemed to pale when the redhead came near.

She had bad skin.

When she spent the night at my house
her makeup browned the neck
of a borrowed T-shirt,
my white sheets, the pillowcase,
and I told you but you didn't care.

You with your Skinny Puppy tapes
and your Bowie posters
and your pledge to want
a strange girl on your arm
until the first provincial one came near
with her exotic vegetable lunches
and the near-sexual thrust
of that dagger-tipped straw
into the glory hole
of her lukewarm Capri Sun

so you pretended to need her
art history notes before an exam,
unaware she and I made out
when no one was looking
and mocked your obsession
with your own profile and how,

no,

you did not look like David Bowie
from *The Hunger* in low lighting,
no matter how long you swore off
eating red meat to maintain
your preternatural white glow.

When you invited us over she
insisted on bringing you ice cream,
vanilla Ben and Jerry's
because your deep-voiced mouth
had never acquired a taste for chocolate
and as she handed the pint to you
in your gloomy apartment,
Dead Can Dance on a stereo in the corner,
I knew she had you
by one flip of her auburn head

so you let the ice cream melt
and posed us like fleshy
blow-up dolls on your bed,
me dark and she light,
me unable to smile and she
unable not to, her cheeks tense
from cheering through life,

and when you told us
to take off our shirts and skirts
and just wear our bras and tights
and pretend to kiss

I hated you for wanting
to seek out and destroy
the mystery in each of us.

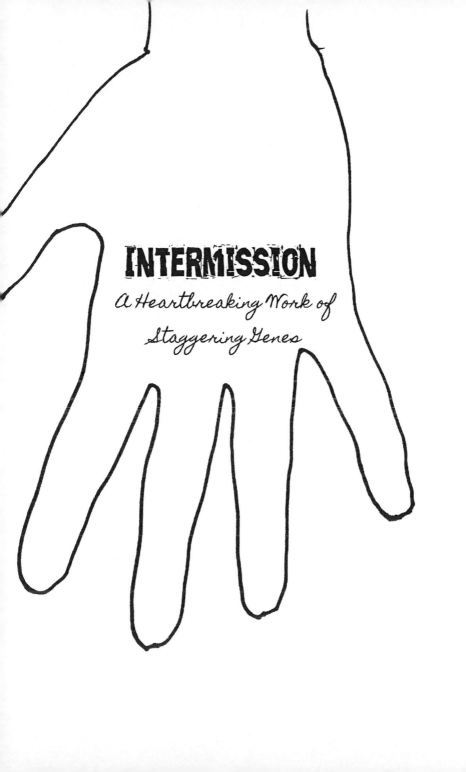

INTERMISSION

A Heartbreaking Work of Staggering Genes

HOMECOMING

You really were too pretty
in our high school cosmos
to care that I wasn't.
Yellow highlights, big breasts,
the kind of fat, sassy lips boys
who listened to Bon Jovi dreamed
of inserting into their favorite image
of the girl who worked
the diner all day then came home
to dole out sexual favors
and white trash pep talks
about holding on to what they got.

At least I never wore my headgear to school,
but I did read Camus during lunch
while you prowled the cafeteria
like a video vixen
eating your handful of tater tots
with the kind of magnetism
even the principal noticed.

When Homecoming and your invitations
from quarterbacks and butt rockers,
science geeks
and the closeted kid from drama club
flooded your locker like smudged doves,
I waited for someone to see past
what I was to who I would become.

Then came Rick on a Polo cologne cloud
with streaked hair and white Keds,
without socks, even in winter,
one Benetton sweater on,
an Esprit sweater tied around his neck.

My first taste
as he ordered cocoa at a football game,
then threw away the Styrofoam
after one sip, of the troubling,
self-aware glory of being rich.
Then came my invitation.
To a real dance with photos
posing under a balloon arch.
His real car.
Probably even a real dinner first,
somewhere with chilled butter.

And you and your mom
thought he was only joking,
your mom with a face
more like a man's face,
and weren't you so lucky
to favor your beautiful father
who pretended to write poetry
at the best strip clubs in Portland.

And wasn't I so lucky that Rick
overlooked certain things?

Isn't that how your mom put it?

How nice I found someone
to overlook certain things,
and how funny you thought she was,
and how sad I felt turning down
my invitation to dance
under a gymnasium floating
with aluminum stars
hung from the ceiling,
close enough to almost wish upon,
close enough to almost touch.

BITCH

Doctors thought you had breast cancer
so I sat with you in a waiting room
until they called you to be X-rayed,
prodded, embarrassed more than usual
for being born with a body that felt like,
from birth, it was set to betray you.

You spoke of the man you really loved,
different than the man you married
who dug hidden packs of cigarettes
out of your rain gutter in the middle
of your lame parties while the man
I married wondered
why I stayed friends with you.

But there's something about
girlhood friendships men
can never really understand.

The fighting, the hair braiding,
the notes folded
into complicated paper flowers,
the way I picked you up
off the bathroom floor Junior year
when the boy we both wanted
chose me.

And there's something about

girlhood friendships women
can never understand.

All those professions of happiness
when I told you tales
of the cherished boy, the dates,
the way his alien beauty
made me more desirable
when he stood so close

and how you hid, and held,
a specific hatred for me for decades,
through cookie swaps and babysitting,
ladies lunches and book clubs,
until the sun announced itself
on a particular summer morning
and you told a rumor
everyone chose to believe,
all for a boy who
was almost worth it
but not quite.

Me,
another man,
an alley late at night,

your words spreading the way
the cancer you ended up
not having spread
in a different woman's breasts

so I couldn't even add my sympathy
to the stack of parties
I was uninvited to,
the phone that stopped ringing,
the desserts we always shared
after salad and Diet Coke lunches
I ordered alone,
the tines of my fork dragging
through the chocolate sauce,
a mark the whole restaurant
turned to see.

THE PSYCHIC AND THE
BOOKSTORE OWNER

We sat like two nervous girls
and ate ice cream sandwiches
in silence in the middle of your store,
waiting for the psychic,

a woman you never told me
was the woman you paid
one hundred dollars three times a week
to figure out the mystery
of how your drunken mother died

so I sat and I laughed and I lied
about having a brother
so the psychic told me about my brother
and I lied about not having two sisters
and the psychic told me
how I would feel in the next life
with two sisters
then charged us both a hundred bucks
for the pleasure of being lied to

and even though you knew
she lied to you too, you called
for other believers to burn my book,
a small town pyre
at the next psychic fair,

the book that brought you
an audience and business
and introductions to the world
of other writers you wanted
to starfuck off the Indie Next list
while your husband bragged
that reading wasn't really his thing
so I sent him *Dandelion Wine*
on the kind of summer afternoon
when Bradbury becomes
everybody's thing
and sent you flowers
when I was in Paris
and your store was doing well
and we should all be celebrating

two women brought up
in Central Oregon soil
who learned to love words
in their own way, anyway,
even as you lit mine with a match
and told the other women
to come closer.

THE SUN WILL COME OUT
TOMORROW

In fifth grade I loved you
more than I could have loved any boy
because you knew your times tables
and wore unicorn barrettes
with pink and white braided ribbons
tattooing through your dark hair
and ate chickpea salad for lunch
while the other girls chewed
peanut butter and jelly sandwiches
with their mouths open

and I think you loved me, too,
and your family took me
trick-or-treating once the same night
your father gave your older sister
a corduroy blazer
because you explained to me
how older girls sometimes
need to be given things for no reason,
and how someday, when we grew older,
we vowed to give each other
things for no reason

then went back to singing
Love is a Battlefield
into your bottle of strawberry shampoo

in the middle of your bedroom,
our sleeping bags arranged
almost close enough to touch.

We bought rubber stamps
to decorate each other's math papers
and turned the dots on our *Is*
into alternating pictographs
of bubbles or hearts
and outlined each other's hands
during art and tried to read
Judy Blume's *Forever* in the dark,

(Like my mother said,
you can't go back to holding hands.)

until the day you came to school
and told me you didn't want to be friends.
No reason. No explanation.
No understanding of how I felt
being dumped in front of everyone
moments before the tryouts
for our school production of *Annie.*

And how I was never going to try out,
the girl who almost cried
during spelling bees
when all eyes turned to me
and I forgot that *r* in February,
but the teacher passed around
the curly red wig to any girl

who longed, center stage in the gym,
to be the girl with no parents
or prospects or place to live,
still so loved
even stray dogs followed her home.

HER EYES WERE NEARLY FULL OF LANGUAGE

You were my secret and I was yours,
even when you sent me
perfumed letters from your year abroad
and surprised me one Christmas
with real chocolates from real Paris
leafed in real gold.

(Remember that time
you were coming for a visit
and sent me a card
saying you were coming
that arrived in the mail
an hour before you?)

We made each other dinner
and bought each other dresses
and we sent each other letters,
though we lived in the same town,
and our boyfriends never guessed
about the nights you shoved me
against my front door and kissed me,
your mouth feeling the way
I imagined my mouth felt,
and we were so much the same,
the same small breasts,
the same young bodies,

only yours smelled like Fendi.

We existed in a year or two
of birthday presents and picnics,
boys on the side
to keep up appearances,
boys in college
to pick for class projects
and boys to memorize
Prufrock in lit class
until we could find our way
back to each other,
and how sleeping next to you
was like sleeping next to something
too beautiful to be real, your
crimson lipstick that somehow stayed on

until the afternoon
you picked me up for lunch,
though lunch really meant
ordering a piece of cake
and staring at each other,
and you told me you were pregnant.

The guy who you let see you
in the shower with wet hair.
(You hated wet hair.)

The guy who inspired you to wear
the velvet cape I gave you
for your birthday

to see a famous cellist
in town for one night,

and you were getting married
and wasn't that exciting
and wasn't I happy for you
and wouldn't my job feel

so important,

holding your groom's wedding ring
in the palm of my hand
until you called on me
to place it in yours.

PART FOUR

The Man Who Was Really a Boy

THE MAILBOX

The night you left
cookies in my mailbox
you assumed no boy
had ever left me anything
even though you taught college
and were almost forty.

That you were somehow new,
that winter night,
and I'd never guess
you grew up average
then chose to stay that way
by the friends you kept
and the girls you didn't,

by your books and records
the same as my books and records,
and how that meant something more
than us both growing up
in a town with one bookstore,
with one record store
where the owner knew our names,
knew we bought Alice in Chains
followed by Elvis Costello until
we both graduated to Tom Waits.

On your muscles you wore his lyrics
tattooed in plodding script,

lyrics to the song
you put on my first mixed CD,
not caring that I was married
and too old for playlists
written in middle-aged cursive
on small slips of red paper,

too old to be seduced this way.

Too old to not know
you put that song on mixes
before and after me,
a girl in the road to your next girl
who waited with her plain face
to hear about the last meal you ate
before you tried to kill yourself,
though I've always been suspicious
of boys who try, and fail, to die
but know how to hold down jobs
and where to score drugs
and how to navigate
complicated recipes in *Cook's Illustrated*.

I really hated the way you called
Anthony Bourdain *Tony*
like you knew him,

like in the city where you cooked
you would have shared each other's
mise en place almost like lovers,
your coolness and his coolness

never too cool
to cancel each other out

as you traded stories
about the one you used for her cookbooks
and the one who cheated on you
and the one who was only joking
with that restraining order,
and how you were only joking
when you tattooed her name
across your chest
because you wanted so badly to belong.

TOY DRIVE

You hated the Disney Princess set,
all the books, crayons, necklaces
that glowed in the dark, plastic tiaras
set with multi-faceted plastic jewels
I picked to donate to a toy drive,

how we fought in the aisle at Costco
while George Bailey wished The Emporium
Merry Christmas on a row of TVs,
no shades of grey
in his black and white optimism,
the bells, the snow,

you grabbing at the princess box,
your big hands grabbing at me,
so disappointed I still believed
little girls loved castles and ball gowns
and that forgotten glass slipper.

Because you were a professor,
in the car you lectured me
on the danger of letting girls believe
they can grow up and marry royalty.

But what about Wallis Simpson
and Prince Edward,

Caroline rollerblading
with John John, arm-in-arm?

What about Lady Di
and the Duke of Cambridge,
and the way you sometimes looked at me,
after you put away your books and pens,
as if I was someone worth kissing awake,
worth searching the kingdom
for her other shoe,

worth holding the night
they killed Diana in that tunnel
and I stayed up until dawn,
my head unable to find
the cool side of the pillow,

a candle lit in the living room
blown out,
the silent vigil between us
while we waited to hear
each other's name in the dark.

COFFEE AND DONUTS

Our first and only trip out of town
on a summer early morning
with the right CD playing
and the right clothes packed
and the train case you gave me
filled with city-girl makeup
and Portland perfume

and didn't I think
we'd make a splash strolling
up and down town with nowhere to go
and the neon rose on the waterfront
ready to burn bright on a night
that was supposed to be our night

away from growing older
and worrying about bills and jobs
and eternal plates of balanced meals

until you pulled over
for coffee and donuts
moments after hitting the road,
though you never drank coffee
and you never ate donuts

but had it in your head
that a trip for me meant
a never-ending bounty

of sugar and caffeine.

The clean racks offered
buttermilk bars and coconut holes
and rows of frosted chocolate

and I let you pick
and I let you pay
and I let you hand me a small white bag
while I held your coffee,

a moment between us that felt sweet
and somehow earned
from all the friends before
each of us who didn't sit
in a car letting us talk

until I joked about your hidden
adoration for rainbow sprinkles
as they fell from our fingers
onto the rugs and you told me
you only stopped for coffee and donuts

because I am the kind of woman
who will always find a man
to buy her coffee and donuts

and something about what you said
and how you said it felt
so real and so true

and so full of the kind of hate
that almost always follows love

I handed you my last bite
and waited for you to start the car.

RIVETS

We fell so far from the afternoon
you punched rivets
into the tongues of my boots

to hold the hard leather
straight against my ankles
because you could not bear
the idea of me getting a blister

so you sat on your floor
in the corner of a room
we tried to turn into something
more than a single-wide trailer
with cop cars scanning the park,
with the nicotine
from some other man's cigarette
staining the walls brown
after you showered,

with the weight of never
having enough money
something you tried to hide
with Fats Waller
on an old turntable in the corner,

with a kitchen cupboard full of figs
and organic toaster pastries
and the goat cheese

you only called *chèvre*,

the keepsakes of fine living
almost close enough to touch

as I waited for you to turn
my boots into something more
than another pair of ill-fitting Docs,

before things
pushed themselves too far,
before the emails
and the restraining order,

the teddy bear you gave me
packed away, the books
and the typewriters gone,

the recipe forgotten
for the cookies we baked
on a rainy day
when you almost listened
to my theory that Carrie Bradshaw
was our modern-day Cinderella,

think slick Mr. Big and the sapphire blue Manolos,

and you almost didn't laugh
as you leveled off
cup after cup of flour
with the edge
of your very sharp knife.

NEIGHBORS

We listened to records on your bed
while his wedding ring
waited to be found,
the neighbor before you
who lost his band years before
his wife died of cancer
in your new bedroom.

Each time I looked at you
I remembered the girl
from high school
who baked banana bread
for any boy she wanted to date,

and how I'm not sure
if she baked in a yellow kitchen
or if I'm just remembering
her youth surrounded
by ripe bananas, by offerings
no boy ever turned into love.

You always offered me things
I never asked for

and tried to convince me
I had an eating disorder
when I didn't want to eat
biscuits and gravy

at your mother's house
because I didn't want to be fat like her

because you looked so much alike
but hated your body
and the way your stomach
alerted the world
to your secret love

for chocolate milk and éclairs
in the Fred Meyer parking lot
under the light that moths
couldn't help but fly
too close to while we sat
side by side and you hoped
I'd someday sit closer,

my mouth full of cream
while I wondered about
your neighbor's wedding ring,
the gold circle you found
while readying the yard
to plant strawberries

so our last summer together
could smell warm and sweet
the way your mother's roses
in the late July heat
smelled like jam,

she your neighbor who wondered
why we were friends

and if you'd end up in a hospital bed
with your stomach pumped again
once you dared to be more
than my neighbor

and I thought you meant
something like best friends
as I pretended to like
your mother's Southern cooking
her glasses of buttermilk,
when all I wanted to do
was move away from both of you

though I never understood why
until you found and pawned
the neighbor's ring for sixty dollars,
a gold show down the street,
the money burning a hole
in your T-shirt pocket
as you asked me what I liked to eat,

if I wanted dressing on the side,
if I wanted to sit close enough
to share something.

PART FIVE

Cougartown

YOU ARE A LOST BOY

and I hope you stay lost
as I watch you from a hotel bar
in a seaside town somewhere
between the East Hamptons
and a Morrissey song.

Outside the wind shrieks like it does
in scary movies about pirate ships
and lighthouses,
me tucked inside a resort
with expensive drinks
and free mixed nuts
as you move your body against the air,

a body that never wears a shirt,
even in this mist, the raccoon tail
pinned to your jeans a striped beacon
I track along the familiar shore.

The other boys I met at this beach
years before you were born
have all grown up,
their rock star dreams,
their poet dreams,
even their pirate dreams
replaced with backaches
and mortgages,
balanced meals and Internet porn.

If every heart is made of roads,
each beat a grid of starts and stops,
pumping boulevards
to get from Point A to B,
the heart of a Lost Boy meanders
like a European avenue,
like an experimental novel,
like a beachcomber unaware
of sand sinking into their shoes,

forgetting to wear shoes like the boy
who held my hand on a beach
under the moon when,
in youth, we did things
like decipher tide tables from a small book,
chart the moon in another,
choreographing our aloneness
to be more important
than any other couple's aloneness.

He was too young
to smell like cologne.
I made a pin for his lapel,
too young for a lapel,
shaped like the moon back
when girls made things for boys
and wrapped these things
in notebook paper.

We listened to the same music.
We used the same shampoo.

We painted our nails black
in a way different
than any other black nails.

When he went away,
like Lost Boys always do,
I carved the name
of the next one in the sand
but the tide erased that name, too,
until the beach became an ocean
of forgotten names,
a sea of fragmented poems,
a memory of so many temporary tattoos
sealed with long kisses,
sealed with promises
folded up in more notebook paper

until the afternoon I saw you
and wondered where you were going
and where you had been.

CANDY BOY

It's so dangerous
what boys can do to sweets,
their hands too warm,
too slick with sweat
to handle anything
with a low melting point,

but you worked behind
the only candy counter in town
so all of us waltzing
towards menopause
had to go through you.

There's something
about women and chocolate,
a calling men do not understand

with their motorcycles
and their metal beer signs
and their shows about Alaska.

There's something about chocolate
not even women understand,
a calling to indulge,

the quiet that always follows,

the Lifetime movie channel,

the extra blanket,
the pajamas,
the lazy thoughts of Colin Farrell,
or at least who Colin Farrell
was supposed to be when his Irish brogue
first hit the scene.

Maybe you,
the boy living among chocolate,
understood in a way close enough
to be called understanding
as you layered white boxes
with chocolate dipped Oreos,
chocolate dipped cherries,
truffles the size of golf balls,
for women on the hunt
for the rich, dark stuff.

On my recent visit
I stalked the glass cases
like the chocolates
had become the audience
and I was the animal inside a zoo
not sure where to focus
but hungry for everything at once,

a blur of dark, milk, white,
a blur of you
with your flop of light hair,
your lips the color
of Gummi Bears.

On my turn to claim my bounty
you handed me a candy
snug in its paper wrapper
without asking,
something different from my order,
something unexpected,
something white with a red center.

Then you offered
a milk chocolate circle
with orange filling.
A caramel wrapped in wax paper.
A piece of taffy with a fractal middle,

my body filling with the aftermath
of such unexpected desire
as you fed me candy
until I could eat no more,

my belly expanded, comfortable
with being uncomfortable,
relaxed in the unknowing
of when the next treat would come.

FOR THE BOY WHO BAGS MY GROCERIES

and knows I like paper.

My bag boy with the messy hair
and the smile stuck
a little crooked to his smooth face
talks about floating the river
with other girls his age
while his large boy hands
always pack the cold with the cold
and never asks why I don't
buy watermelon on days
when everyone buys watermelon.

He asks me to float the river,
not knowing I'm married,
not knowing I can't swim,
not knowing I'm old enough
to be his mother,
not knowing I'd insist
he wear sunscreen on his flat abs,
not knowing I'd pack him protein snacks.

Hummus. Peanut butter.

The boy who bags
never says things like,

Jeez, you eat a lot of vegetables,
on weeks when I surrender
to the effort of asparagus
or convince myself
to reexamine the pomegranate.

On low afternoons
when I try to conceal multiple trips
to the bakery sample tray,
all those plastic cups rimmed
in sickly sweet frosting,
all those tiny plastic spoons
I hide under my purse,
the boy who bags my groceries
removes the refuse of my sugar rush,
the spoons marked with red lipstick,
without comment or complaint.

On days of cramping
I sneak a slice of cake
onto my peaches
and he packs the cake
like precious cargo
between my gum and my tabloids
while, together, we ponder
why Kanye married Kim.

I ask if he think it's true,
that Robert Wagner
killed Natalie Wood
as I imagine floating

in an inner tube
through the middle of our town,
a picnic arranged on his stomach.

I think my grandma liked her,
he says,
and the river dries up between us

until I put my thoughts of him
back in the gilded cage
I open each Tuesday afternoon
in his check-out line,
the little bird of hope
that sings its secret song
only we can hear
above the mechanical remix
of barcode blips,
the cleanups on aisle three,
the leaking package of meat,
the coupon that won't scan.

SEASONS

Talking to you made me feel
the way Ali MacGraw felt
when her Harvard boy
zoomed her away from school
in his MG TC in *Love Story*,

something about your blond entitlement
so alive,
so American,
so destructive,

your biologic imperative to conquer
every woman in your path
as one night away from home
placed me in front of you at a bar
celebrating your college graduation.

At the bar you were Kennedy
as a senator tonguing your way
through each girl in line
to get closer to you,
in line to commemorate
the night you turned their way,
noticed the passing pose
of pair after pair
of glossed lips, tank tops,
hair that arranged itself before you
in amber waves. So patriotic,

how their blondeness
met your own
with the unspoken agreement
to celebrate the song of each other.

Your body not really the body
of a man, but grown past the body
of a boy as my forty-year-old thighs
practiced the art of sitting like a lady,
knowing the less I noticed,
the quicker you'd notice.
And what a boy you were,
a boy who knew
how to get me in trouble
with that crowded mouth
that lost its baby teeth
years after Kurt Cobain died,
your perfect row of constellations
lined up to spell my name
before asking it,

to reveal a life of stock options
and ski vacations, sex in frat houses
careening towards date rape,
bottle after bottle of whipped cream vodka.

That rise of golden hair,
that menace you pushed
from your brow
to only have fall back,
resounding yellow shockwave,

your perpetual motion,
your raised flag,
your promise of a secret
almost too dear to whisper.

(But didn't you take the first chance
to whisper, to come near?)

You smelled like trouble,
your smile carrying with it
the odor of coercion.
Odysseus the cunning bringing you
one step closer to Ithaca,
your testosterone a jangle
of warning bells, your brutal preen
nearly intoxicating
as you introduced yourself
with a hum in my left ear.

A smell of cheap beer,
flavored alcohol turning your lips
fruity like a child's lips,
even your sweat sweetened
by the rush of hormones
you had no reason to ever rein in
as I wondered how many eggs
still waited to ripen
in a quiver in my body,
my basket already emptying itself
for thirty years,

and why your breath in my ear
made me think of eggs
and baskets and Easter,
that grassy renewal,
that jelly bean exhale,
that rush of first blossoms
pushing through the aroused earth
to brave any light they can.

EPILOGUE

MY GANG

My gang formed at fifteen,
seeking each other out
the way trails follow rivers,
the way steel-toed boots
and dark trench coats
seek each other in a sea
of Benetton and Esprit, 1988.

We grew up from the ponderosa
and lava, the Sears Toughskins
hardscrabble boys out-turning
each other's Indian burns
on the playground
and the girl who loved them.

My gang was the kids who wore
Magic Marker-ed jean jackets,
Metallica, AC/DC bleeding
in their mothers' wash,
which followed with a beating.

I have always loved poor boys
with worn jeans and messy homework
for what they never forgot to give me.

Sending roses to a Prom Queen
is too easy. Impermanent.
Two decades later and I still

have a box of riches I carry with me.
A Denny's napkin
stenciled with Cure lyrics.
A quarter Deric gave me
so I would always be able to call home.

The pencil Josh handed to me
when I dropped mine in math class.
I remember his blue eyes,
his skateboard, how he told me once
while we waited after school for the bus,
I think you are so cool...
Freshman year I shared my lunch
with Rex because he had nothing to eat
and no one at home who noticed.
My gang was malnourished.

Rex would steal cassettes for me,
Talking Heads, Siouxsie and the Banshees,
and I would pretend a whole sandwich
was too much for me,
then starve the rest of the day,
beatific in my hallucinations
for one candy bar, one potato chip.

I would pretend I always drank
two cartons of milk, fifty cents,
but shoved one tiny blue box his way.
Every day for a year,
as our fingers barely touched,
it felt something like prayer.

John's grandpa molested him
in a Deschutes River Woods shed.
He told me this, but only once,
late at night, because he knew
I would never mention it again.
Sometimes he cried in art class
and blamed it on being stoned
and only used pencils
so nothing smeared as his tears fell.
When I turned sixteen
he drew me a picture
of a wishing well
and taped three pennies to the back.

Jason's mom died of cancer
so we adopted him.
Once a week my mom
washed his clothes
and made him chocolate pudding,
the whole box, and he ate it
and watched MTV, pointing out
how all the girls
were only half as pretty as me.
He wrote me love letters,
with some words misspelled,
and Pablo Neruda hopes
he could ever write as well.

My gang didn't wear black
to blend in, but to stand out.
We painted spider webs

on our lunchboxes and clothes,
smoked cloves,
watched *Clockwork Orange*
and *Brazil* on continuous repeat,
didn't eat meat,
were always called fags and witches
between class in the halls,
could not catch balls or give speeches.

We longed to invite Brian De Palma
to our dances and pull a *Carrie*
on the blondes in back,
the top-drawer party girls
with perfect curls and bubblegum,
and doily dresses
ringing their store-bought tans.

My gang, Kris, the two Jasons,
Sky, and Eric explored
caves out on China Hat,
midnight flashlight tag,
though we were never Satanic.
Most weekends we dyed
each others' hair black
while debating the intricacies
of music and comic books.

They were all my boys,
these wild things
with sleek bodies full of rage,
filled with blood, with semen

that never knew where to go.
The Outsiders searching
for an older brother like Patrick Swayze
to take care of Ponyboy Curtis
and the rest,
let them watch cartoons
and eat cake for breakfast.

The danger in loving a wild boy
is that they almost always love you back,
but only until their life turns tragic.

My gang moved away
when they dropped out,
discovered big cites, drugs, sex.
Every time one of my boys moved on,
I cried for the holy trinity of loss,
my lovers, my brothers, my sons.

I have been told I love too deeply,
but this is the only way
to hold fire in your palm,
force the world to stop
and watch you burn,
to carry the wildness of youth
inside your older bones
with your box of treasures,
your faded love letters,
each memory ruptured and luminous,
brilliant and broken.

ACKNOWLEDGMENTS

Thank you to the boys, and girls, who make up this book. Memory is a subjective thing, often colored by good kisses and bad breakups. In no order, thank you for the mostly happy trip down memory lane Deric, Rex, Sky, Chris, Blanton, Padric, Dan from California, Jason Simmons, Jason Dodge, and Professor X. The rest of you, thank you for the poems.

Tommy Gaffney, thank you for asking me to be the opener for Michael N. Thompson at Tony's so Eve Connell could find me.

Thank you to William Akin for the first read of this book a few years ago, and for the best advice about the book—advice I didn't take but now would. (Duh.)

Greg Gerding, Eve Connell, and University of Hell Press, you rock, obviously.

ABOUT SUZANNE BURNS

Suzanne writes mostly in bed, mostly in the late afternoon. When her stories aren't appearing in the *Chicago Tribune*, she scans Pinterest for cake recipes to enter in local county fairs. She is always working on a new novel.

by GREG GERDING
The Burning Album of Lame
Venue Voyeurisms: Bars of San Diego
Loser Makes Good: Selected Poems 1994
Piss Artist: Selected Poems 1995–1999
The Idiot Parade: Selected Poems 2000–2005

by LAUREN GILMORE
Outdancing the Universe

by ROB GRAY
Immaculate/The Rhododendron and Camellia Year Book (1966)

by JOSEPH EDWIN HAEGER
Learn to Swim

by LINDSEY KUGLER
HERE.

by WRYLY T. MCCUTCHEN
My Ugly & Other Love Snarls

by MICHAEL MCLAUGHLIN
Countless Cinemas

by JOHNNY NO BUENO
We Were Warriors

by A.M. O'MALLEY
Expecting Something Else